THE BIRD

PREETHI RICHARDS

Contents

Contents

Contents

Prologue

THE BIRD is the collection of prose and poetry. It is a collection of mixed emotions in which Poetess tried to convey different types of feelings using Metaphors as literary devices.

ABOUT AUTHOR : Preethi Richards a nature poet whose central theme of poetry revolves around nature.

She made her debut with "NAKED LOVE" and continued her journey through most celebrated book

named "SOLITARY SOUL - sings poetry". She resembles an old soul living in young body with her poems.

She is from KARIMNAGAR, TELANGANA State.

1. THE DAYS

There were the days i understood

Thousand meanings from a single word,

And there are the days where I cannot understand a single

meaning from thousands of words,

Am I ignoring the long written sentences?

Or Am I lost in the river of words that people say?

Should I believe the words? For words are numerous and

infinite!

Or should I believe the people? And again people are

numerous!

My brain in incapable of deciding.

So I left my condition to this Nature,

To the early sunrays,

To the misty clouds,

To the blooms of garden,

To the chirping of birds,

And to the Jingles of pets,

I leave it to them, which can make me understanding.

~preethi.

2. BEAUTIFUL WEEKEND

I am standing by the sea side
The sea surrounded by its shores
The moon shining brightly
Above the deep blue waters

I hear in the middle of nights
The hitting of waves towards the cliffs
It lures me to discover them
The mystery behind these waves

I sit down by the shore
On the silky sand listening
To the tales of these
Waves, mostly about wars

To give it's approval
To these tales the wind
Blowing and throwing
My hair in all the directions

They were like a lullaby
To me, and i slept

Under the blue sky
I spent the most beautiful weekend.

~preethi.

3. MEMORIES

I was walking in the evening when sun was setting down gently,
the sunrays hitting and sinking down calmly.
I was walking on the small path
heading towards the destination
that's unknown
It has been my habit of walking and
getting lost in the gardens,
drenching in the rains and
loosing myself to the chirping of birds
But today is different,
today my brain is heavy and
my shoulders are burdened by something
that I can't figure it out and
the same path lead me to this place.
The Railway station which is crowded with lots of people and
everyone has there own type of story of their life....
I understood now that I am burdened by the "MEMORIES "
and I think every human is bound by the same.

-preethi.

4. PIONEER

Can i be a pioneer of a different society which is of having non mechanical minds and less logical ones with more goodness.

I am living in the imaginary world of people whose emotions are not felt deeply by themselves

but are rather connected to the materialistic things.

Happiness is justified with the costly items and not with the real simple things.

People here almost forgot that they are living and were always mad at one or other thing.

I strive to build a little for myself the close centric space where people of good souls could enter,

interact share energies with each other and always be thankful for that they are living.

And living is what we all need.

-preethi.

5. BROKEN

Something is always broken,
Nothing is linear in this mighty world,
Every body has a worn out cell
Detached from its body,
That's a break,
Every roof is made up of a broken tile,
For it makes a beautiful home,
Every tree has a broken twig,
Where it replaces with new leaves and stems,
Every one has a broken promises
which are always ready to move out of the door,
Sad! Perhaps! But this is what we need.
Excessive is always a poison,
Excess cells makes cancer,
Excess stems breaks a tree,
And excess promises worn outs a Man from interior,
Remember, something is always broken,
And some things are always fixed.

-preethi.

6. SICK

I am sick to this mode of living,
To this life not with the sickness I posses but
rather the sickness that lies in this method of living.
There is neither the art of living in it nor
the efficiency in the patience of defining death.
Merely there is void created by this elicit which
further on became a drift from the real possessions.
And I am sick at it.
I need an another one.

~preethi.

7. SUFFERING

What the suffering is? Where does it come from?
Suffering comes for the people who has hearts and no brains?
Or it comes in the air and spreads with our inhales and
exhales?
Oh I wonder about these suffering!
And I do wonder that it is an aberration made by
human resisting the peaceful life.
And what is life like to the people who say they suffer?
Life is an entire misery and unforgiving incapability of
existence.
They cause themselves to suffer and let their souls burn in the
fire
with the least knowledge that they are the cause for their state
of minds.

-preethi.

8. BORED

I am bored as hell,
Bored with this routine life,
What's worse , I guess I am falling
Out if love these days,
I'm becoming colder than people
And colder towards people,
I can't trust people either!
I guess there are only
Few people left in this world
Who could understand the words and
could speak the true feelings in words,
Only few souls left who could understand the love,
the intimacy and act accordingly of humanity.
When I am acknowledged with this fact,
I am bored as hell.

~preethi.

9. CHANGE

By and by little by little I changed,
I changed my way of looking at people,
I changed the way of understanding them,
I changed my way of looking at the things too,
My eyes could now recognise the change that
always been but I couldn't look at!

My mind now understood that
People are too cold to handle,
Less with humanity and more with thirst of money,
I had to gain a lot of strength to take this
This type of reality which always existed
But somehow this sensitive soul never understood until today!
And this all never happened suddenly
but it took some days, weeks and months
to summit the strength within me.

-preethi.

10. GARDEN

Come into this garden dear,
I am at the gate all alone
Inviting you for the evening tea,

Come into this garden dear,
It's always open for the visitors
Like you, whom I envy.

Come into this garden dear,
Where we can chit chat
Until the bats fly above us tonight.

Come into this garden dear,
For a breeze carrying the
Smells of the climbing roses and Jasmines,

Come into this garden dear,
Sit under the tree and unburden
Your issues and pains here.

Come into this garden dear,
For I am always awaiting along

With these garden to help you,

Ease your mind dear,
Pour your heart here,
Redefine your life here.

Come into this garden dear!

~preethi.

11. MOUNTAINS

The mountains are calling and I must go,
I have been wandering every where and anywhere,
But I am unable to find them

I have been through these fields
And Meadows for thousands of times,
Wandering and being lost in them

I have seen thousands of sunrises
And sunsets on that mountain,
I can still see them when I close my eyes,
I can see the summer flowers
And rainy patches covering the
Paths of mountains, with whom I made a crown

When I open my eyes everything is gone,
Lost in this crowded towns,
Lost in this foggy vehicles,
But I must go, my mountains are calling me.

~preethi.

12. TIRED

I am tired, am tired of
Explaining about my feelings
Am tired of hearing the excuses,
My body is tired,
My brain is tired
Of running to and fro in this timeline,
I am tired of expecting the love,
Love that can heal my wounds,
I am tired of searching for it
Without the lamp in my hands,
I am tired of searching truth
In this desert of lies,
I am tired of searching for a soul
That matches mine in this overcrowded
Ignorant masses,
I am tired now, even my heart is tired of,
Even my aches doubled up,
My soul worn out,
Even my faith in this world is tired!

-preethi.

13. TRUE COMPANIONS

The wind moaned at me,
As if moaning in between my legs,
More like screaming and less like swaying
It seemed, grinding up the bones.

I fastened my way towards the farm house,
I could see mu dog longing for my visit,
The closer I drew, I could
Watch the glare of it's eyes,

The droplets of rain started to pour,
Come closer come closer,
Seek shelter in comfort,
Come into me said my home.

The thunder striked the sky into two,
While my porch door opened slowly
Splintered wood like toothed jaws
I could feel the tiny branches beating my hands

They are my true companions,

My plants and trees awaiting me,
My dog longing for my sight,
I could feel this nature in my veins.

-preethi.

14. THE PLACE

It's the place I come again and again,
I love to revisit no matter what the time is
At the edge of my soul it drives me

I visit there to unveil my happiness,
To fill my unfulfilled wishes,
To fill the void that left in me.

This is the place where my happiness
Grew, grew like a tree in the backyard
With roots building like memories.

Here I was left with foot prints,
Of the unforgotten, they brew
In the storm of hourglass

Here I set my foot again on
This ground, where I should plant sone seeds
The seeds which ought to grow,
The seeds of HOPE

~preethi.

15. WHITTLED DAY

I whittled the day away,
With the dull edge of my sorrow,
I sat still simply observing the
Slowly moving shadows around me,
Why do all the people carry
So much of Luggage and baggage
On their shoulders?
Though invisible I can sense it.
Why do they carry all the
Seasons of life on a single day?
Keeping their thoughts in lock and key
Imprisoned, indeed lost the key
They had spent their lives
Like an individual fighting in
The battle ground with their
own demons and their own thoughts
I passed a good day's rest
Wrestling With this unrested thoughts,
A day wasted well enough!

-preethi.

16. SPRING

Ah spring I was never sure
That I matched your thoughts
But I am always sure that
Yours matched mine.
But it's beautiful that
We are on the same page
In the book named Life.
You remained as hymns and praises
In the sights of poets and saints
You are the vows and promises
Of the sad and broken hearts.
You holded my heart,
When I am left alone in this contemplation
I watched the world through the closing doors
Where you holded my heart filling with hope.
Ah spring you filled my life
Same like you coloured the trees
As calm as it, you are not just a season
You remained my life.

~preethi.

17. HAPPINESS

There is a light in my heart,
That sometimes burns me down
And the other times it is the only
source of my illumination.
In the rainiest nights it shows me the path
In the darkest winters it keeps me warmth,
It is the only spark that remains in me
Keeping me still alive,.
Loving still and leaving off still
Remains the same for me
Though the words differ
The meaning remains same,
Holding on and moving on
Are the same lines in the spectrum
Just with different alphabets
Yet with similar pain,
It's all about the time
That blinds us,
That fools us for the kindness we crave,
For the happiness we strive.

~preethi.

18. I AM

I am like a country with no citizens,
I am like a train that never had passengers,
I am like an abandoned road who never takes,
I am like a large tree which had no bird visitors,
I am like a caged bird lost in between these iron rods,
I am like a kid lost in this mighty world,
I am like a snail with no shells,
I am like a stranger with no shelter

~preethi

19. NEVER BEEN

From even childhood, I have never been
Like any other kids,
I never seen the world like they did,
My eyes never watched the happiness
Like the other people did,
There were the passions that
Gave me happiness, not the people!
I didn't have the voices of joy
To remember in my memories,
Whatever my little heart
Loved, was and is loved by loneliness,
And all alone I was left Alone like this.
I grew up more or less like this!

~preethi.

20. SITTING ALONE

I would like to sit alone, whether it may be
A broad daylight, or in middle of the day
Or else in the dusk and dawn.

I would like to sit alone at the seat
Of the window corner,
Looking at the strangers passing by.

Initially I used to sit and immerse
Myself in the future thoughts
Imagining like meeting someone,

Someone who is alike, consuming
My time with the happiness,
But the immersion only left me with a scar,

I would like to sit now and watch
Watch people with mechanical smiles
And artificial togetherness,
And I would like to laugh at them
For I experienced the backstabs of these closeness!

~preethi.

21. STILL ALIVE

Suddenly in the middle of night
I feel the pain in my chest,
A stabbing pain of knife
That continuously stabs me,

The pain with no single droplet of Blood,
The aches which has no cure yet
There sits something on my heart,

A heavy weight which can neither be
Seen nor lifted up by anyone,
It crushes me down to the earth.

I find no therapy for this wounds,
I find no drugs to heal this aches,
I find no person in rescue,

But I live like this still laughing and
Yet not letting anyone know that
Am suffocating from deep within.

-preethi.

22. WITNESS

Is there any witness for
What does the final breath contain?
The words always left unspoken!?
Or the favourite songs?

Are the words about the final goodbye
Or the farewell?
What does it contain?
The thoughts that were buried?
Or the life that is left unlived?
Or the things that haunted?

Does it contain the oceans of secrets
That were buried deep within for the
Entire life?
Or an ambiguous summarization
Of memories and days?
What does it contain?

It perhaps contains the love,
The memories of loved ones,
The life lived and life unlived,

Memories of people whom they are
Going to leave,
And everything remained unsaid
And wrapped in the blanket of death
Leaving it as mystery!

-preethi.

23. HELP ME

Help me open a window,
A window for my new life
I could see all the beauties of life,
But my reality is a barrier

Help me open that window
For the life I strive is before
My eyes to be lived,
And i crawl here to reach.

Help me open the window,
Windows of happiness
Where my soul to be heard
Of all the gloom it had,

Help me open this window,
Where the sun and moon
And the stars strive and look
Forward to give me a new life.

Help me!

-preethi.

24. A QUESTION

There is always a question in my mind,
Why does this pain never end?
Pain and creativity seems synonymous
To me, both are never ending!
I was and still kept asking my life
Why should I put so much effort
In being like the other people?
It just laughed at me.
With this pain I turned towards
The creativity and art
From where I pulled the
Point if happiness,
The happiness in fact drove me
Believe me!
Both pain and art are synonymous
They are on the same page of life.

~preethi.

25. RECOGNISE

When I meet someone like me,

I try to recognise them the longing for their peace,

Their mental conditions, their dilemma, their source of happiness,

their point of numbness, their strings of heart and everything that creates them, I try to trace their memory of Ashes on their face,

and what else do I need to know to connect with their soul?

~preethi

26. BEFRIENDED WIND

Often I noticed that this wind doesn't care much about my
problems,
When I yell at her about them she just smiles and
blows my hair with her speed
And moreover
She visits me in a good mood always.

Such a befriended WIND...

~preethi.

27. SPREADING

If everyone takes spreading happiness and
kindness as their own act of responsibility then
Imagine how wonderful this earth gonna be to live on?
Why not that simple act of giving roses,
smiling at the person down the street,
wishing a person on their routine hectic schedule,
bringing some cakes and bakes to the home.

Inviting neighbors over home to the dinner,
Picking up the elderly people
Helping them cross the roads and streets and
dropping them at their door step.
How gently the world will move if this acts becomes
everyone's routine?

~preethi.

28. REDEFINING

This is me like someone who finds themselves,

I want to discover the curiosities like

"what would it to be to wake up in

the new city with new hope",

What it would be to travel the journey for months which would

usually take a couple of days, so that i could feel the long enough

secrets of that location,

I just want to find the "HOPE" In every moment

and in every simple thing of life,

There are the conditions of my life like sitting in the boredom

routine of life,

Shutting down myself in this bored bedroom,

And questioning this personal lesson

that arise daily,

But Yes, I am not going to answer this questions which

fade and shift but inviting this new questions to solidify,

This is me redefining myself.

Yes, this is Me.

-preethi.

29. BLESS THIS WIND

• 33 •

Bless this wind which touches me while am walking in this ground,

with the greenery around me.
Let that wind touch the flowers which are at tip of the tree,
Let that wind enter and exit the thick bushes around me,
And let that wind enter my soul and fill me with that all purity it's been through.

Bless that wind.

~preethi.

30. COMPANY

• 34 •

In many times I prefer to have my own company,
In other times too I prefer to be alone if not with my own
company
but at least with the company of nature,
Nature and loneliness are alike they provide me a space
to keep things for myself,
And I admire this things rather than dwelling on my own
kind of sickness which I had no friends left that creates a void
and that void later forms a blackhole in my memory and heart
and I know there is no coming back from this type of trauma.

~preethi.

31. THE LAST DAY

When will be my days lovely?

When I say lovely I heard the universe laugh at me, and at my foolishness

I thought I asked for more

The word "Lovely " meant for me not the riches or luxuries

But I long for a day which is so simple like me doing my own works by my own hands free of any aid unlike a handicapped one,

Here I remember and cry upon a fact that I always had a life of an uncertified handicap with uncertain future,

I wish all my body parts are free of ailments and I wish I could use them properly the way they were designed for,

I wish my mind and heart a piece of freedom, because they always run an errand and leave me wretched,

I wish them to stay calm and hear my grievances, atleast for once in my wrecked life!

I think this type of lovely day will be a day of grief and sympathy!

The last day!

-preethi.

32. I WISH!

I wish I had power in my hands,
Some sort of power that could change
And not a change of a huge one
But a little change, a small change
In which I can give power to little girl children to reach out to
the schools,
A change in their lives where the head weight from logs will
be lost and replaces by the books,
I wish to give them books to read and am saying just to
"READ" not
for the scoring though!
The books to read which gives their imaginations fly,
I wish I had power to let them fly!

I wish I had a power to make a little change in the opinions
of the
parents of girl children that Every girl deserves to fly,
And Let the education be their wings,
Let us not chop them down,
I wish I had a power to make a impact on them.
I wish I had a privilege to look into the happiness of every
young girl child

The happiness in their eyes when their hands are free from the
household chores and replaced with crayons and colors,
I wish I had a power to watch their faces bloom like a rainbow
loom,
And their smiles like sunflowers in the garden.
I wish I had a power!

~preethi.

33. BY YOUR NAME

Call me by your name,
This is how my love is,
The transition from mine to your's is a far long way
which had built upon a strong belief,
It is the echo of my heart which had picked up the phrases
from your life,
My head had habituated some of your habits so strong
that those acts became a personified tract of my living,
That's why I say,
Call me by your name!

~preethi.

34. A MORNING

See, there will be a morning in life, that one morning after many years of despair nights,

disappointing events, and many dark nights of unbearable pain,

an irrepressible longing to live, will announce the fact that all is finished

and everything had come to an end, a closure of darkness and the fresh light of rays of that morning saying that every suffering

has no more meaning now than happiness.?

~preethi.

35. ABSENCE

• 40 •

What was once present is an absolute absence now,
Perhaps,it's a real proof that time is always a flowing form,

Why do we always eliminate a rational proof
Of fact that we are loosing most of our time
in making poor and dumb decisions?

~preethi.

36. DUSKY NIGHT

In the dusky night, A house in the abode
Behind the rustling of Peepal trees,
We gather on our Pial the three of us
Grandma, grandpa and Me.

Grandpa laying on the cot on the Pial
Grandma on the rocking chair,
Holding my heart towards her Bossom,
Sings the lores and Myths of the village.

She weaves the myths of hidden treasures
She sings the folk songs learnt from her
Grandmother and stories heard from her
Grandfather,

She tells the tales of the haunted woods,
The tales of the kings and Queens,
Their victories and defeats, Our
Pial is filled completely with the memories,
Like the wind filled in the fields,

She had a magic spell which creates
A myth into a realistic picture,
Which I dwell later on in my years,
She made my days with the essence
Of MYTHS AND MAGICS.

~preethi.

37. I PRETEND

• 43 •

I pretend not to care about the people who carry their brains
with the distinguishing mentality of the looks people posses,
the Colour of their skin tone, the values of their costumes,
the amount of makeover they have on their faces and bodies.
Why?! I pretend in vain where the whole world is at the
darkest side,
while I pretend not to have the impact on my tender heart
in which I always lose.

-preethi.

38. SUPPRESS

• 44 •

I am always suppressed not to talk about my concerns,
not to speak about my prospects, not to learn about my
authorities.

Whom do I blame?
Does the blame normalize the things?

I think a person's individuality has been under
the tremendous amount of pressure of this society.

~preethi.

39. WRONG CENTURY

• 45 •

May be I am born in a wrong century,
May be I should have been born
"When there is a life to live"
May be I should I have existed
When it's possible to experience
the natural lives around me,
May be I should be at the time
When life is little slower and little peaceful.

~preethi.

40. QUIET MORNING

It was a quiet morning,
A moment of meeting between the
Garden tipped heads of wheat
And mist of rising dawn.

I went on an early morning walk
Through these golden fields
Which are waving in the
Calm weather

I walked through the
Tiny Paths of our village
Which will be soon crowded
By the wagon and cattle

I walked through the weeds
And the patches of wild
Bushes which are just awake
With the morning dew

I heard a greeting
"hello, how do you do"
from the top of the mountains

And the hills

Do you know who called me up?
No one just those beautiful mountains.

~preethi.

41. THEY ASK

• 48 •

If they ask, "what do you do in this world? "
I simply can answer,
I am Left in this universe all alone!
And you know what I managed to live here all happily!
Because I am acquainted with this little sparrows,
The busy running squirrels on the branches,
The morning hastening hens,
The lovely butterflies in my messy yard,
The tiny insects and bugs roaming on plants freely,
I am left with all of them to endure,
And I feel like I am never alone,
But I am a lone one in this Universe.

-preethi.

42. TELL ME

Will there be something like a day?
A day in which I can wake up happily
Towards the chirping of birds
On the branch of the tree towards my window pane,
Will there be something like a day
In which I can fly like a bird reaching
The skies?
For which can I have wings?
How that feel can be?
Has that feel has something
Great like a some great places which
I heard of?
Who can tell me about it?
Oh the sailor from the seas
Could you please tell me?
Oh the wisemen from the
Countries
Could you please tell me?
Will there be something like a day?

~preethi.

43. MIDDLE OF THE NIGHT

From even childhood, I have never been
Like any other kids,
I never seen the world like they did,
My eyes never watched the happiness
Like the other people did,
There were the passions that
Gave me happiness, not the people!
I didn't have the voices of joy
To remember in my memories,
Whatever my little heart
Loved, was and is loved by loneliness,
And all alone I was left Alone like this.
I grew up more or less like this!

-preethi.

44. SKY

When I go up through the
Golden fields in the sun setting rays,
I have climbed the hills of view
And looked down the world.

My folks who are passing by me
Down the hill from the works
Laughs at me asking
"Is the sky your relative or something? "

I laugh and say "oh yeah, it is! "
The sky is relative for all of us,
The voyage for the birds
And the dreams of humans,

It is the friend of a lonely writer,
Companion for the moon lovers,
Host of millions of stars,
And number of birds.
Sky is indeed a relative of mine!

~preethi.

45. AM LOOKING

I am looking for something,
That is lost long ago,
Long ago perhaps before
I was born.

I am looking for it in the
Corridors of my house,
House that's been haunted
By the demons of memories,

I am looking for it the
Crowds of people,
People of very insane and inhumane,
And nothing much more

I am looking for it in the
world of strangers eyes
In their thoughts, in their
Words that were left unspoken.

I am looking for it in the
Great sailors of the sea,
In the great knights

In the warriors.

I ask all of them
Do they know what I need?
Do they know the address
Where I could find it?

~preethi.

46. HOW FAR

How far we have come
Down the track, the lane
This road twists and bends
Like a snake.

The whole way was
Filled with our giggles
And laughs and gossips
The time was running in a slow motion.

How beautiful the days were?
My dear friend! I envy them
The evening meetings
The kindly gestures

Sharing the aroma of
Our cookings,
Having tea together in the
Gardens.

We never ran behind the
Time, we never lived like this

Before, we are living now
In a complete abandonment.

~preethi.

47. TIMELESS NIGHTS

Timeless nights passed
By the company,
The cold company of
Rusty thoughts.

The rainy nights are passed
Passed by the company
The cold company of
Faint memories.

The memories of farm hands
Whistling, and cattle dogs
Barking kicking off the
Dusty earth.

The days were in the
Company of cattle, farmers,
Plants, fields and
Old gardener

Were now just in the company
Of strange spiders who incessantly

Weaving their webs against
The harsh winds.

There is no sight of
The dusty roads, the cowboys
The sounds of Bullock carts
And no laughter.

Where am I living?

~preethi.

48. YOUNG

When I was young
But happy I remember
The days of me running
Running barefoot on the
Ground that is completely
Filled with new greens of the year
I remember the other kids
Ran along with me happily
Flaunting,
We gathered at a point
That's pre decided and
Voted by all of us,
We gathered and talked
About everything and anything
And kept ourselves amusing
We played hide and seek
Only to find out the
New mysterious places
And call ourselves as
Knights of the war
And the warriors of the game.
We had races with our
Bicycles and the

While troop rided with
The hope to win the race
As if it was an olympic race.

• 59 •

How pure our souls were!
How happy we were!

~preethi.

49. IS IT HARD

My eyes we're filled with tears
The vision in front of my eyes
were blurred,
It's hard to see a way out of it
Isn't it?

My life has a veil, like a bride upon it
There are people in front of me
But i couldn't see them,
It's hard to see a way out if it
Isn't it?
My shoulders were burdened
By the ways I pretend to be
Lived and the way I didn't
Live my life, it's hard to see
A way of it Isn't it?
My thoughts are weighed
Like a rock upon me
And i couldn't find a way out of it
It's hard to see a way out of it
Isn't it?

-preethi.

50. A SEA

Timeless nights passed
By the company,
The cold company of
Rusty thoughts.

The rainy nights are passed
Passed by the company
The cold company of
Faint memories.

The memories of farm hands
Whistling, and cattle dogs
Barking kicking off the
Dusty earth.

The days were in the
Company of cattle, farmers,
Plants, fields and
Old gardener

Were now just in the company
Of strange spiders who incessantly

Weaving their webs against
The harsh winds.

There is no sight of
The dusty roads, the cowboys
The sounds of Bullock carts
And no laughter.

Where am I living?

~preethi.